# Time Management

## THE SMART WAY TO HAVE MORE FREETIME IN YOUR LIFE

Dr. David Carter

## **Table of Contents**

| | |
|---|---|
| Introduction | iii |
| Chapter 1: The Concept of Time Management | 1 |
| Chapter 2: Why Managing Our Time is Difficult | 6 |
| Chapter 3: Ways to Better Manage Our Time | 11 |
| Chapter 4: 50 Helpful Time Management Tips | 15 |
| Chapter 7: How to Organize Your Life | 38 |
| Chapter 8: Always Remember | 44 |
| Chapter 9: Overview | 47 |
| Conclusion | 50 |

# Introduction

I want to thank you and congratulate you for downloading the book ***TIME MANAGEMENT- THE SMART WAY TO HAVE MORE FREE TIME IN YOUR LIFE.*** This book will truly transform your life in more ways than you could possibly imagine. This book is for all of us who struggle with managing our time and for those of us who always seem to be racing the clock. This book is for those of us who always feel like we never have enough time. This book is for those of us who feel like time is our enemy. With this book you no longer will view time as your enemy, but more so as your natural friend.

This book contains proven steps and strategies on how to become truly efficient in managing your time. This book provides helpful tips and hints on how to better manage your time. This book will discuss how family, friends, and life itself can be pushed under the rug when time becomes inevitable. This book will further push the boundaries on normal time management tips. It will include a how to section in which I will explain how I created my own time management tips. These tips will make you feel more confident and efficient with your time use. This book will explore the misconception of time and give you a whole new perception. This book will allow you entrance into a whole new world, where you can learn to control time.

Here's an inescapable fact: you will need determination and patience to gain the skills to better manage your time. You must be determined in maintaining good habits and make sure you stay on schedule. You must have patience, because it might take some time to really understand and put into effect the time management tips that are discussed in the book. You must have patience, because time can feel overpowering, but soon you will have the power in your hands. Those are just two of the main traits you need to possess, and if you don't have them now....Well they can be learned through experience.

If you do not develop better time management skills, then please do not get discouraged. As stated earlier, gaining these skills could take some time, hence why you need to be patient. However, do not fret you will succeed in gaining those helpful tips and managing your time. You will be able to work, see your family and still have time for your friends as well. You will even have some time for yourself. You could even start a hobby or host a weekly book club meeting. The sky is the limit.

*Time Management*

It's time for you to better manage your time and be able to live life to the fullest. It is time for you to open the pathways of a calmer and more freeing type of lifestyle. It is time for you to lessen your stress and gain perspective. Are you ready for this adventure? You better have said yes! Here we go...

# Chapter 1: The Concept of Time Management

*Where did all the time go?*

If you are like me then you feel like you are always racing the clock. You feel like there is just not enough time in one day to get everything done. You feel tired, and exhausted trying to keep up with the daily demands of life. You try to manage your time, but it just doesn't work the way you wanted. Let's face it time has its own schedule and we just have to quietly follow along. Yes we have to follow along, but we can do it to our own beat.

There is a way to better manage our time. However, first we need to understand the concept of time management. It seems simple enough, but you would be surprised how many people often are misled on the true meaning of time management.

According to the businessdictionary.com time management is defined as:

"Systematic, priority-based structuring of time allocation and distribution among competing demand s. Since time cannot be stored, and its availability can neither be increased beyond nor decreased from the 24 hours, the term 'time budgeting' is said to be the more appropriate one."

Hmm there are some pretty important words in that definition that we need to look at closer. For instance, "time allocation" and "distribution." What do those words mean in this context?

First off "time allocation" can be easily summarized as the amount of time that is being used by certain activities. These activities are what make up your day. So let's look at some different activities that make up our day.

**Activities that make up our day**

Waking up

Getting dressed

Making breakfast

Going to work

Making dinner

Eating food

Cleaning

Walking the dog

## *Time Management*

Folding laundry

Exercising

Watching TV

Driving

Going to the bathroom

Sleeping

Those are just a few activities that could make up your day. Did you notice how seeing your family and/or friends was not included? This is simply because most of us are not managing our time well enough, and we don't make seeing them a priority. Let's go back to the definition again, the word "distribution."

We need to discuss how "distribution" plays into the concept of time management. Obviously we aren't distributing our time well enough if we cannot even see our family and /or friends. There needs to be a change in how we perceive our time and what gives us the upper hand.

## Time Management

So now that we understand the concept of time management we should be able to gain a new perspective. We know why we need to effectively manage our time, but maybe we have forgotten what poor time management leads to.

If you look at the list made earlier in the chapter, you noticed friends and family were not included. This is because we are so overly concerned with everything else that friends and family get pushed to the bottom of the list or are not even included. Sometimes we cannot make the time to see or talk to our family/friends, but I would say that is a lie. You can make time, and you can better manage your time. You just need to get into a certain routine.

Once you have a strong routine down, then managing your time will become like second nature to you. A strong routine is the foundation of organization and managing your time. Now we discussed the concept of time management, but we barely covered why time management seems to be difficult for us to understand. We didn't really go over any main reasons why time management is one of those challenges that we face daily.

*Time Management*

In the next chapter we will go over some main reasons why time management can be difficult for us. We will break those reasons down and give a positive reinforcement for them. We will discuss ways in which you can change how you manage your time, so you are more effective in doing so.

Ready for the next chapter?

# Chapter 2: Why Managing Our Time is Difficult

*It just seems impossible…*

Managing time is a difficult matter, but one that can be easily understood. We already briefly went over how managing our time can pose a problem, but we didn't go over the main reasons why managing our time becomes this unbeatable challenge. It always feels like we are racing the clock or fighting against time. People always seem to be complaining that they never have enough time or simply don't make the time to do the things that they want to.

It is wrong that we don't have time to see our friends/family, and that we barely have the time to keep up daily with ourselves. It is sad that we make other things a priority in our lives. I am guilty of it as well. I prioritize things that really shouldn't be. It isn't right that our family/friends are last on the list. It is true that our family have seen us through thick and thin. It is true that our friends have been there during moments of triumph and despair. They have done all of this for us, and we can't even spare some time for them? It doesn't seem right .It doesn't seem fair. This is because it isn't...

Let's discuss the main reasons why our family/friends don't receive much time from us. If we look at the main components of what makes up our time, we should be able to get a clearer picture.

## **Components that make up our time**

Our job

Our significant other

Our pet

Our home

Those are just four components that make up our time. I hope these components seem familiar to you as well. There could even be another component that you could add as well. Make your own list, if this list does not reflect your current situation.

Let's further break these components down.

*Our job.* It seems fairly obvious that our job would take priority, but let's look into that. We need a job to have an income, to support our lifestyle, and to guarantee our future. Our job is what keeps us away from our loved ones, and usually gives us unnecessary stress. The one thing that we need most is what takes us away from our family. We need a job, we need a way to live and we need to do this effectively. We need to be able to leave our work at home. We can't bring it back with us, for it will only complicate matters.

*Our significant other*. Our significant other usually takes up a lot of our time as well. Whether we are having dates or just having conversations. We spend an incredible amount of time with our significant other, and that is perfectly normal. However, we need to make time, possibly reduce the time with our significant other, so we have time to see our family. Sometimes you need to make a change in your life to gain better positives.

*Our pet*. I don't know about you, but my pets usually take up lots of my time. I have a bunch of cats, a dog, and fish. The cats always need their litter box cleaned, or they are always knocking things down. The dog needs to be taken on walks, and trained as well. The fish are probably the less intensive animal to take care of. For all I need to do is make sure their water is clean and they have plenty of food. Now it is hard to reduce our time with our pets, but we can create a routine. For instance maybe clean the cat litter box every other day or three days, instead of every single day. There are other ways to reduce time in that component as well, but honestly our pets don't take too much of our time.

*Our home.* I just recently bought a house, and I feel like all of my time is geared towards improving the house. I am always cleaning, rearranging, and sometimes even painting. Now, even if you have had your house for years, you still are spending a lot of time cleaning it. So a way to better use our time in this component is to once again get into a certain routine. Possibly clean the house every weekend, instead of every day. I know it can get crazy, but we must stick to a positive routine.

Another component that could be taking up our time are our kids. I don't have any kids yet, but I imagine when I do my time will be gone before I know it. Kids will take up a lot of your time. You will need to be doing things for them instead of yourself, and you won't have a lot of time left over. Kids also are messy, so you might be cleaning more as well. It is hard to reduce time with your kids, because they are your family, but don't let this component get in the way of others. Allow yourself some breathing room.

## *Time Management*

Honestly out of all of those components I would say only two are the real reasons why we have issues managing our time. These components would be our job and our home. You could also include our kids if you have kids as well. It seems these components are what are manipulating our use of time. We need to figure out a better way to manage ourselves.

So looking into those components we can see how managing our time can become indeed very difficult. It is hard to find ways to reduce our time spent with other activities, but is a necessity. As already stated, maybe that list of components did not fit your situation. Maybe you have a completely different list of components. If that is the case, then use your list. Make it your own. Do whatever it takes to succeed in managing your time.

In the next chapter we will discuss a few ways on how to better manage our time. We will go into ways that can help us better ourselves and our situation.

Ready?

# Chapter 3: Ways to Better Manage Our Time

*It is time to manage...*

So we discussed what time management was, why it is so difficult, but now we need to focus on ways we can efficiently use our time. Ways to reduce our time from the already mentioned components can take us on a different path. I hope to lead you down that path today.

**<u>Here are a few ways to better manage our time.</u>**

Get into a certain routine

Develop good habits

Don't overstress yourself

Make priorities and keep them

Have goals and stick to them

Let's break these ways down even more. Because they are a little vague, aren't they?

*Get into a certain routine.* You need to make sure that you have a certain routine down. I am talking about, a routine for the morning, your work day and even your evening. So a routine for the morning could go like this... Wake up, make coffee, make breakfast, do half hour of exercises, feed pets and pack lunch. Wow, that is a lot of things to do in the morning before work, but you can see how they all coincide. A certain routine can make you feel happier, and even make you more successful in the long run. If you have a routine, then you have something to rely on every day. This gives you consistency, and allows you to better manage your time.

*Develop good habits.* It is important that you develop good habits as well as keeping them. For instance, make sure you don't bring work home with you. Do you know what I mean by that? I mean don't take your work frustrations out on someone who doesn't deserve it. We are all guilty of it, and it is hard to have that separation, but not impossible. Another good habit, is making sure you eat all your meals, and get everything you want done. This goes with the previously mentioned tip about getting into a certain routine. Other good habits, obviously try not to smoke, or over drink. You can see how if you are a smoker, then this can take up a lot of your time as well. I know many smokers are always wasting their time outside smoking, and seems like they always need a smoke break. This is not an efficient way of managing time.

## Time Management

*Don't overstress yourself.* This is probably the most difficult to do. Everyone gets stressed and how they deal with it varies. However, you must not let the stress overtake your life and further steal your time. Sometimes when you are overstressed you don't want to see your family/friends, because you are overly stressed about something. For instance, maybe you are stressed about something at work, this causing you to not want to speak with your family or see them. Your mind will be on other things. So you need to clear your mind, and be able to work through your issues.

*Make priorities and keep them.* This is also very important to keep in mind. If you make something a priority, then you need to stick with it. So make your family a priority, so then you will be able to see them and you therefore will make time to see them as well. It is a mental stimulation. If you have it in your mind that something is a priority, then you will automatically make time for it. Other priorities include certain goals, friends, work, etc. Make your own list of priorities, and see where it takes you.

*Have goals and stick to them.* This goes with the other tip on making priorities and keeping them. Certain goals need to be kept and improved. For instance, a goal that could

## *Time Management*

deal with work, or even a family member, should always be remembered. You could make a goal that you speak with your mom every other night, or every weekend you could make a goal to see your friends. By making these goals you are taking control of time itself. You are better managing your time in a simpler and more efficient way.

All of these are vague ways in which we can better manage our time. They give us an opportunity to expand our current situation with a new found perspective. The next chapter will discuss actual specific tips and ways to manage our time. These tips will focus on all different aspects of our lives. We will discuss tips that can help in your personal time, your work time, and even your recreational time.

# Chapter 4: 50 Helpful Time Management Tips

*Wow that's a lot...*

So now we will discuss specific tips and hints that can help you better manage your time. These tips will expand on all aspects of your life. Are you ready? Here we go...

(These tips come from various websites and articles. Some were found in a Forbes article, but most were created by yours truly.)

### 50 tips

1) Be grateful. Don't always complain about never having enough time, because I know you do. I always complain as well about the time issue, but instead be grateful you have time at all. Don't focus on the negatives, but the positives of the time you do have. What will you do with that time? That is the question you need to ask yourself.

2) Start your day right away. Don't allow distractions or procrastination to occur. If you start your day early, then you don't have to end the day late. If you are at work, then try not to allow distractions to

## Time Management

waste your time. Start your day as soon as you walk into the office, don't allow small chit chat or other things to distract you from your goals.

3) Value your time. If you value your time, then others will to. If they know your time is important, then most likely they won't try to waste it on silly things. Make sure you are using your time effectively and are able to succeed. Don't waste your time.

4) Ignore email completely. This might be specific for say an office job, but can also be helpful when you are home as well. If you ignore email, then you won't be distracted. Imagine how easily email can distract us. One little email could take our time away, in more ways than you think. Once you open that email, then the contents will be in your mind for the rest of the day. Can you see how that could possibly affect you and take up your time? Most likely it could negatively affect us.

5) We are all equal when it comes to time. Remember that everyone is dealing with time issues as well. Not everyone has all the time in the world. So don't think that you are different in that respect. We are

all equal. We are all struggling with the same time challenge.

6) Use your time for things that matter. Don't waste your time on pointless things. Remember what is important to you. This goes along with your priorities. Your family and friends should be one of them! Make sure that you keep your priorities and that they don't change.

7) If you are procrastinating, then ask yourself why. Why are you procrastinating? Are you afraid of the task that has been asked of you? Is something upsetting you at home? Is anything bothering you? Sometimes we push away what is bothering us, and it comes out in another form. A form of procrastination.

8) End your day at a set time. This could be more specific for work, but is helpful none the less. Make sure that you are ending your day near the same time every day. For instance, make sure you leave work by 5, and don't stay later. ( I know sometimes work demands we stay late on certain occasions, but it should not be every day!)

## *Time Management*

9) Sleep. Another important tip. If you don't have enough sleep, then you will be cranky, sleepy, and unable to complete certain tasks. If you don't get enough sleep then you won't have time for other things. You will miss out on a lot in life, if you don't get enough sleep.

10) Stop using social media websites. Or I should say limit your use. I know it is crazy of me to ask you to completely go cold turkey on these sites. I am guilty of it to, as I am always checking my Facebook as well. So limit your use, and make sure those sites are not ruining your life or wasting too much of your time. I know social media websites are a major distraction, and a huge time waster.

11) Do a time checklist. Write down everything you use your time for, and clock it in. Sort of like clocking in at work. You will then see just where the majority of your time is going. You should then be able to adapt and change the way you are using your time. You will become more effective with your time use.

12) What constitutes time well spent? You need to ask yourself this and figure out your true priorities. Make a list so you can see how you rate things.

## *Time Management*

13) Who drains your time? This might be a difficult question, because it is hard to find the answer. It could be your significant other, work, or etc. Once you figure out who is draining you time, then you need to figure out why. This could be an obvious answer, but you still need to ask yourself.

14) Limit what drains your energy and time. Once you figure out what is draining your time, then you need to limit what is draining it. You need to figure out a way to manage this and come up with a solution. For instance, if work is draining your time, well, you can't really limit your job. However, you can gain a new perception on it and accept the reality.

15) Don't let a half an hour fly by. I know many of you, and myself included, think oh it is just a half an hour I can ignore it. However, don't because time is time. You need to use the time you have and don't let it pass you by.

16) You need some down time. Don't always burden yourself with everything else in your life. You need to have some down time, and time to relax. Just a few minutes even, if you can't have more. Maybe try meditation or breathing exercises. You could

## Time Management

even try coloring. This is a new fad, where adults use coloring books as a stress reliever. I have not tried it yet, but have heard good reviews nonetheless.

17) Take mini breaks. If you take mini breaks, then time won't be as daunting. You have more possibilities. After all, everyone deserves a small break every now and then.

18) Factor in how long something will take. If you know beforehand that a task will take an hour then you can better manage your time. If you foolishly think the task will only take a few minutes, but then takes an hour. You aren't very prepared, are you? So really think about the task at hand.

19) Make deadlines for yourself. Do you like working and knowing you have a tight deadline? For some it can be more stressful, but for others it gives them motivation to get things done. If you have a deadline then you can plan for the rest of your week, so you make sure that you make that deadline. Do whatever works best for you.

20) Are you forcing things to get done? Take a break and realize things will get done eventually.

## *Time Management*

Stop forcing yourself and making more unnecessary work for you to do. Sometimes you just need to accept the inevitable.

21) Here is an interesting one. Spend your time instead of your money. Some of us are so willing to spend money, but we need to think about spending time instead with our loved ones. This often gets forgotten.

22) Have a calendar marked with your activities. Once you have a calendar then you can see these activities clearly marked, and you will be able to further plan your day. This will also serve as a daily reminder for you.

23) Wake up earlier. If you wake up earlier, then your day will start sooner. You will have all this extra time, and you will be able to find more uses for it.

24) Use an organizer. If this means an electronic organizer, or even just a paper one, either way have it so that you can be reminded of the tasks at hand. An organizer could be post it notes, a calendar, or even a tablet with important dates included.

## *Time Management*

25) Learn to say no. Sometimes we just don't know how to say no to someone. They will ask us to do something, but we are already swamped. If you keep saying yes, then you are losing your time. If you said no, then maybe you would have more time to spend with your family.

26) Make sure you have a clock in front of you. Sounds silly, but you should always have a clock in perfect view. It helps you manage your time better. It gives you better perspective.

27) Don't fuss about unimportant details. Sometimes we get caught up in insignificant details, and this causes us to lose track of time. We are obsessing over something, which is truly insignificant.

28) Ask for help. If you have too much on your plate, then unload and let others help you. For instance, at home if you are too tired to clean, then perhaps ask your significant other to help you out.

29) Put similar tasks together. By putting similar tasks together, then you are able to get things done quicker. Your day won't be so drawn out.

## *Time Management*

30) Start your day with the most important work. If we start out with the most important work, then it will for sure get done. However, if we leave it last minute then most likely it will be pushed aside for later. This will become even more tedious for you and detrimental.

31) Clear your mind of negatives. If you keep dwelling on the negatives, then you will not be able to get anything done. Or you won't be able to get things done efficiently. If anything you will be half assing your work. This simply meaning, not giving it your all, and being lazy.

32) Manage your energy, just not your time. Sometimes if you take on too much, then this can quickly drain you. If you are drained of energy, then you just won't have the time to get everything done.

33) Keep your eye on the prize. Don't just see the tasks at hand, but see the end goal. See why it all matters in the end. Once you have this goal in mind it will be easier to accomplish these tasks. You will feel like you have a purpose.

34) Be conscious of the amount of time you spend on TV or electronic devices. I know that I spend a lot of

## Time Management

time watching TV, this taking away my time, when I could be spending my time with my family or friends. I need to make the choice to change my behavior. What about you?

35) Exercise. Make sure that you are exercising, because exercising helps to keep you healthy.

36) Eat healthy. Make sure you are eating good balanced meals, because then this helps you stay healthy as well. You need to be healthy in order to take on all of the tasks that require our time.

37) Use your weekends. If you need to use your weekends for getting things done at work, then do it. You need to use your weekends efficiently. Get other things done as well.

38) Clear the clutter. Make sure you have a clean environment. If it is messy, then you will be focused on that instead of the task at hand.

39) Carry your to do list with you at all times. Make sure you have it visible. This way you will never forget what you need to do, and it is within reach at all times.

## *Time Management*

40) Don't over schedule yourself. This goes along with making sure you don't take on too much, but carries the same meaning. If you have a schedule, then you won't be over scheduling. Remember to be organized.

41) Get things done early. If you get things done early, then you are able to free up more of your time. More time allows you to get more things done.

42) Take control of your day. You should know exactly what you want to do before you leave. You should have it all prioritized beforehand.

43) Call your family once a week. Make sure you get into the habit of talking or seeing your family once a week. Sometimes life gets crazy and we just can't stick to this expectation. However, talking to your family once a week can fortify your bond and make you stronger in your efforts of success.

44) Remember to breathe. Sometimes life gets so crazy, it is as if we have forgotten how to breathe. Perhaps we get overburdened and forget every day activities. These every day activities could include, showering, eating, and /or grooming.

## *Time Management*

45) Don't forget the little things. Sometimes we forget the little things that make our life so incredible. This could be the feeling of accomplishing a task, the feeling of seeing our child fast asleep, or even the feeling of making a wonderful meal for the family.

46) Communicate your wants and needs. If you communicate your wants and needs up front then time should not be an issue. If you know what you want to do in the beginning, then you are ahead of time so to speak. You are able to succeed.

47) Plan ahead. Make plans for the future, so you have time for other tasks. Make plans with your family and friends. Know that you have the time to complete those tasks.

48) Use time management tools. For instance, calendar, organizer, post it notes, or etc. All of these tools can help you get back on track. They can help remind you of what needs to be done.

49) Manage yourself. Time will never change, but how we manage ourselves can. So make sure you know yourself and are able to adapt to the demands.

## Time Management

Make sure that you are able to handle everything you have on your plate.

50)     Remember we only have one life to live. So don't waste it. If you remember that, then managing your time will come easy to you. Make sure you remember that, and are able to make priorities. Never forget what is important to you.

Wow 50 helpful hints and tips right there for you to use. All of them are different in various aspects of your life. All of them can help you better manage your time. Regardless of these tips there are important concepts for you to remember.

Remember that time will never change, for it cannot! Time is ever moving, just like our lives. However, we can manage ourselves which in turn helps manage our time. We can make sure that we are continuing to be healthy, and making good choices. We need to make sure we are exercising, eating good balanced meals, and getting enough sleep. All of these seem obvious, but to some, they are not even remembered.

You need to be healthy before you can do anything else.

*Time Management*

In the next chapter we will discuss how to keep up with time and see our family. We will discuss how you can plan events and activities that will further help you manage your time and be able to see your family.

Are you ready for the next chapter? Here we go

*Time Management*

# Chapter 5: How to Keep Up With Time and See Our Family

*It is time to plan...*

We have discussed the concept of time management, ways to better manage our time, but now we are going to discuss one major tip in managing our time. We need to learn how to plan. In the previous chapter some of the tips focused on organizational habits and routines. Remember, how we discussed using post it notes, a chalkboard, white board or even a calendar? All of those are great ways to keep up with time and plan our day! So now we need to focus on the planning aspect of it all. So what does that really mean? Let me break it down for you.

If we don't plan anything out, then nothing will happen. So you need to make it happen by having a plan. Make sense? If you don't plan your day, then you will be losing certain aspects of time. Imagine if you have planned your day, then you would have planned time to call your mom, or stop at the bar to see your friends. You need to have a plan and go through with it.

## *Time Management*

Here are a few easy plans that you can make for yourself. These plans will help you keep up with the daily demands of life and being able to see your family.

### **Easy Plans to Make**

Call your mom and/or dad every week

Call them around the evening, 7PM

Have dinner with your family once a week

Make a special dinner for your significant other

See a movie with your friends

Have dinner with your friends

Go dancing with your friends

Go to the bar with your friends

Now these are simple plans that you can make easily throughout the work week. Here are a few more plans but these center on the holidays or special events. We know how holidays and special events allow us to connect more freely with our family and friends.

*Time Management*

## **Easy Plans to Make For Holidays or Special Events**

Make plans to decorate the Christmas tree with your family (If you celebrate Christmas, if you celebrate another holiday instead, then allow your family to be part of the celebration.)

Take a trip to Washington DC to see the National Tree and festivities

Go see a Christmas musical with your friends

Throw a Christmas Eve party

Make Christmas Eve dinner for your family

Wrap presents together with your significant other

Make holiday cookies with your kids (Again, if you have kids, and if you don't then you can make cookies with your significant other and/or family.)

Throw a New Year's Eve Party

Go bowling on New Year's Eve with your friends

Throw a birthday party for a member of your family

Make a fancy dinner

## *Time Management*

These many examples can help you plan for your holiday events with your family and friends. Remember there are many other activities you could plan for, but these are the most common. If those examples don't follow with your religion, or something of the same nature, then make those plans your own. Change the wording and make it into something you would want to do.

Now we discussed various examples of how and what to plan for your family and friends. Now I know sometimes plans go awry, because of work or other life events. It is ok, that is part of life. However, if you have to cancel plans remember these points on how to address the subject.

You don't want your family or friends to think they are not important to you. So you need to calmly address the topic by using these important helpful tips.

**Ways to Address Having to Cancel Plans**

Explain why you had to cancel

Remind them of how important they are to you

Ask them how they are doing

Suggest another day and time

## *Time Management*

End with "thank you for understanding"

Some of these suggestions might seem more suited for a business setting, but you can adapt and use them in other situations as well. The key point is that you make the person feel valuable, and let them know you value the time you have with them. You also want to bring up another time and day, so that you can try to see them again.

There are no guarantees that you will be able to keep all your plans, but at least you are trying. By trying you are managing your time in more ways than one. You are taking control of your life and making your priorities matter.

Time is always fleeting, but you don't have to be racing against it. You can make the difference by organizing yourself, planning, and allowing life to happen. Time frequently interrupts our lives, but it doesn't have to. We don't have to keep allowing it.

Make a difference in your lifestyle and see how that difference changes everything in your life.

In the next chapter we will discuss how to make that permanent change and allow us the chance at success. We will go over the different ways of how to make a change and maintain that change.

# Chapter 6: How to Make a Change

***Be the difference you want to see in the world***

I know making a change in your lifestyle can seem very difficult. Changing in general is difficult for all of us. Whether you are changing jobs, becoming a mother, or entering a new phase of your life-change can be daunting and stressful. But guess what! It doesn't have to be. Don't let the change consume you. Take control of the change that you are facing or that you are creating.

What kind of change am I referring to? Obviously I am referring to change how you manage your time, and other elements of your life. Managing your time doesn't have to be difficult, but in fact can be a fun and a rewarding experience. If we look at what we need to change and what we want to change, those are two different things.

We **need** to change how we perceive and manage our time. We **want** to change time in general. The first thing we can learn to do, but the second thing is impossible. We can want many things, but wanting something doesn't make a change in our lives. You cannot change time in general. The entire concept of time is hard to change, but you can change your perception of it.

We don't have to be afraid of time and change. We should welcome it with open arms and an opening mind. Time doesn't have to control us. We can learn to control time. Wait, what? Yes you heard me correctly we can learn to control time through our very own perception of it. If we see time as daunting, and stressful, then time will become a bothersome element to us. However, if we see time as normal, part of life, and are able to control it, then time will become an accepted element to us. Which would you rather have?

I would rather have time as an accepted element, than a bothersome one. Let us look at ways we can change our perception of time and be able to feel more in control of it. We need to make the change.

## **Ways to Make a Change and Learn to Accept Time**

You can learn to understand time

Have a calendar nearby, so you can write down current plans

Make a habit to get up earlier than usual, so that you can get more accomplished

## *Time Management*

Perceive time as a friend, rather than an enemy

Perceive time as natural, rather than as daunting

Allow yourself to see how time affects you

Imagine if time didn't exist, how would you be different?

Close your eyes and do some breathing exercises

Remember you shouldn't be afraid of time.

Those are just a few creative ways to further accept time and to change your perception of it. You may have realized many of the examples were mind exercises, calm breathing, and the use of organizers. Hopefully some of those were able to put the concept of time in perspective for you. Hopefully you were able to make a change.

With any change, you must be open and aware of the consequences. However, with this change, I don't think there will be many negative consequences. If anything this change has expanded your mind and created a new world for you. Well, maybe that is a bit of a stretch, but it's pretty remarkable. Once you are able to perceive time as your friend instead of your enemy; life becomes remarkable.

## Time Management

Your stress lessens, your mind opens, and you begin to feel satisfied.

What do I mean when I say satisfied? Do I mean happy? Content? Well sure those words could be used to describe your state of mind, but I would rather say I mean you are satisfied in your life. You start to feel accomplished. You feel like time is just another part of your day and not something that you fear. You feel on top of the world, so to speak. You feel invincible. Doesn't everyone want to feel that way?

Yes they do, but it takes a new perception and acceptance to get to that state of ecstasy. It takes hard work, determination and patience to succeed. Do you have all of those traits? If not, you can easily learn them.

In the next chapter we will be discussing how to make some most needed changes in your life. We will discuss ways to better organize your life, and allow you the possibility of success. This will reference just another change that you should be able to make for yourself- The change of life.

Are you ready for the next chapter?

# Chapter 7: How to Organize Your Life

**It is so messy…**

Life is complicated. Hell, let's be honest sometimes life can be a big ass mess. We try to make the best of it, but sometimes you just can't. You have to deal with the cards that you have been given. However, you can deal with it by changing your life and organizing it. You can make that difference by focusing on what is really important to you, and then everything else will fall into place.

Organizing your life might take some time. Who knows what you are dealing with? Everyone is fighting his or her own battle, and it would be ignorant of us to think otherwise. So when you begin to organize your life you need to consider these tips.

**Ways to Organize Your Life**

Find your priorities

Set certain habits

Get in a certain routine

*Time Management*

Remember to keep in contact

Don't let stress control you

Think of the positives

Make plans and do your best to keep them

Make sure your home is clean

Make your bed

Take time for yourself

Those are just a few helpful tips that can hopefully allow you ways to further organize your life. Some of the tips might seem redundant, but redundancy never hurt anybody. There is a reason why they are mentioned again. Everything has a purpose. Remember that.

If we look at a few of the tips, and slightly break them down we might come across a pattern. For instance, make sure your home is clean. How can you be organized when the place you live is a complete mess? You have to clean it, or else it will control you. You will be so focused on the mess that time will fly right by. This rings true for the other tip of making your bed after you dress for work. You will feel much more organized and content coming home to a made bed, than a messy one. These might seem like trivial tips but they do all add up. One thing to another, then to another, and then bam you have let your life become a circus.

If we look at the other tips, such as don't let stress control you and think of the positives.... We can see a pattern being created. Can you see it? The pattern is you. All of these changes in your life have to come from you and have to be kept by you. Also you will notice many of the tips are referencing back to your mind. You must have an organized mind as well.

Let's face it; our mind is probably the biggest mess we have to clean up. So many people struggle with stress, depression and other ailing mind sicknesses. We cannot forget to organize our mind. Our mind controls us, so to speak.

Once you have made a change in your mind, in your life, and have allowed yourself to become organized-you will see the difference. Being organized allows you more time to do the things that you want to do. It gives you the option and the possibilities.

It is important to have organizational skills in life. Now this could mean making sure the house is clean, to organizing files at work, to even making sure you have spices organized in the cabinet. All of these are simple but crucial organizational habits. Once you get into the habit, then it will become like second nature to you.

Organizing one's life is not as simple as you would think. You see you have to be able to break down certain barriers and boundaries. You need to be able to set goals and make sure you achieve them. Organization takes hard work and patience. Are you up for the challenge?

Here are some organizational practice exercises

1) Go into your kitchen and look in your cabinets. Do you see the different spices, junk food, and /or soups? Are they messy or neatly arranged? Most likely they are messy, with so much to do in life, we hardly have the time to neatly arrange our food. However, if your cabinet is neatly arranged, well then bravo! Now organize your cabinet and see how long it takes you. How long did it take? I would imagine not very long. The purpose of this exercise was to show you that organizing your cabinet can be done easily, but organizing your mind will take time. Also this was to show you how a messy kitchen/cabinet can affect you. I bet you didn't think it could.

*Time Management*

2) Now I want you to go to your closet. Don't go to the one with the clothes on hangers, but the one that has the clothes folded up in drawers. Now is there a specific pattern to these clothes? Again, sadly I bet there isn't a pattern. I want you to take all your clothes out of the drawer and organize them. Find an organizational pattern and stick with it. You could organize the clothes by color, by style, or even by preference. This exercise was again to show you how things that are messy in your lifestyle can affect your mind.

3) Now I want you to go and look at all of your shoes. Well, if you have many. I have quite a few, so I can easily do this exercise. Anyways, look at your shoes and once more, I want you to try to find a pattern. Did you find a pattern? No? Shocker, except not really. We really are not as organized as we think we are. So once more, I want you to organize your shoes by some type of pattern. The pattern could be by size, by color, by style or even preference.

Those were just a few simple organizational practice exercises. I hope you found the common concept I was trying to reveal to you. Simply saying, we are not organized. We need to be. Take a look at yourself, look at your life and see ways that you can improve it-see ways in which you can manage and organize your time better.

Becoming more organized doesn't have to be so difficult, and yet as these exercises revealed-we just aren't organized. How can we manage our time better and see our friends/family if we aren't organized. Simple. We cannot.

We need to be organized, so we can manage ourselves and our time better. We owe it to ourselves, don't you think?

In the next chapter we will be discussing just a few important things to always remember about time. We will go over different ways of acceptance and further bring up the illusion that time is daunting. You can control time and you can manage your time better. Don't let the misconception control you.

Are you ready for the next chapter?

# Chapter 8: Always Remember

*Keep these things in mind....*

Throughout the book we discussed various ways of managing our time, ways to organize our life and ways just in general to succeed. However, there were several important factors I always included in every chapter to help you better understand the concept. This chapter will focus on those important factors, and help us remain in control.

I bet you already have a clue of what I am going to be discussing. I have mentioned these factors throughout the book. In fact you might have found it slightly redundant. I am going to stop you right there. The reason why the factors were mentioned several times was because of their significance. If you found it redundant, think again. Everything mentioned in this book has a purpose. Do you know what that purpose is? TO HELP YOU.

However, I digress... Here are some important factors to always remember

**Important Factors**

You can learn to control time

## *Time Management*

You can change your perception of time

You can become organized by changing your habits

You can get into a certain routine to start your day off right

You can make time to see your family/friends

You can be successful at home and at work

You can become organized by simply cleaning your home

Clear out your mind

Think about the positives

Remember you have the decision to either see time as your friend or enemy.

Make the right decision

Use a calendar

Use a type of organizer

Those were the main factors I wanted you to understand and furthermore value from this book. I hope you were able to understand the meanings and concepts that I have included. As already stated some of these factors may seem like common sense, but you'd be surprised how many people don't already know them. Some of these factors might seem odd to you. Maybe you are still trying to wrap your head around my comment about changing your perception of time, or maybe you are just confused. Well, don't be. Take the time to reread the sections of this book that confused you or were unclear. I promise you will be able to succeed.

In the last chapter we will do a brief overview of everything we already covered. This section will be good for those of you who are still lost or are unsure of certain concepts.

Here we go.

*Time Management*

# Chapter 9: Overview

## *What have we learned?*

You made it to the last chapter of the book!!!!!!!!! Congratulations. Now in this chapter we will do a quick overview of everything that was already discussed in case any of you got lost.

So in the beginning we talked about the concept of time management, and how people perceived it differently. We expanded on the theory that time management is all in how you perceive it and how you live your life. We then focused on reasons why managing our time can become a challenge. I had several examples and tips for how to fix that scenario.

In the middle of the book, we discussed how we can manage our time better. I gave 50 helpful hints and tips that focused on the problem at hand. We broke those hints apart and further analyzed the meaning. We then discussed specific ways in which we could plan to see our family members and friends. Again, I provided you with a list of helpful examples and tips. We then discussed how to make that so needed change in your life and how that change can better suite your needs. We then focused on ways to help organize your life in general. I provided you with practice exercises and examples as well.

Towards the end of the book we focused on more examples of time management, important factors to remember, and helpful hints. We discussed the different perceptions of time and how you have the choice of how you perceive time in general. We discussed the misconceptions of time, and how viewing time as your enemy obviously hurts you in the long run.

Throughout the entire book we focused on the nature of time, how time interferes with our lives and how we can make the change to be in control. I discussed methods and ways for you to live happier lives. I mentioned hints along the way that should have encouraged you to manage your time better.

Overall this book was aimed at the goal of giving you a concept and allowing you to change all on your own. Of course this book was able to help you get started, but ultimately you need to do the rest. The rest is up to you. You need to make sure that you keep up with your routines, that you have good habits, and you allow yourself room to breathe. All of it really is up to you.

## *Time Management*

So remember whenever you are worried about time, dreading something, and feel like you are racing the clock…..You have the power to make a change. You have the power to make a difference. It is all up to you. I have provided you with hints, tips, and examples. I have given you the push you needed, and now you need to do the rest.

Don't let time control you. Don't let time pass you by. Don't ignore your family and friends because you haven't managed your time properly. Gain those organizational skills, get into good habits and make a difference.

Time waits for no one…

# Conclusion

Thank you again for downloading this book ***TIME MANAGEMENT- THE SMART WAY TO HAVE MORE FREE TIME IN YOUR LIFE.*** I hope this book shed some light on the misconception of time and provided you with better ways of managing your time. I hope you enjoyed this book immensely and it was able to give you some clarity. Hopefully this book was exactly what you were looking for. I hope this book did more than help you, but gave you a new way of life.

I hope this book was able to help you manage your time better. I hope you were able to feel more organized and you were able to take control of your life. I hope you were able to see your friends and family more with the help of this book. I hope the examples and tips made sense to you. I hope the practice exercises proved essential in your understanding. I expect you have a broader concept of the term time, and that you are ready to become more organized. I believe that you were able to feel more confident in your habits and ways of managing time.

## *Time Management*

The next step is to practice. Remember I said earlier, that you need determination and patience to succeed. Organizing your life and managing your time better will take some time, but I believe in you. Do you believe in yourself? I really hope you do. Remember, you must organize your mind, before you can organize anything else. Things can get complicated and messy, but you have the power to escape it all. Remember that time is your friend, and not your enemy. Time is not daunting, but rewarding. Take control of the time you have and efficiently manage it.

Finally, if you enjoyed this book, please take the time to share your thoughts and post a review on Amazon. It'd be greatly appreciated!

Thank you and good luck!

www.ingramcontent.com/pod-product-compliance
Lightning Source LLC
Chambersburg PA
CBHW070406190526
45169CB00003B/1142